WHO THIS BOOK IS FOR

This book is for:

- Aspiring entrepreneurs who want to build a consistent income using systems on Amazon

- Individuals who value long-term stability over quick wins

- Professionals seeking location and time flexibility

- Business owners who want to transition from operator to owner

- Those who understand that building a real business takes time and effort

If you are serious about building something sustainable — this book is for you.

WHO THIS BOOK IS NOT FOR

This book is not for:

- People looking for "get rich quick" schemes
- Those unwilling to follow compliance rules or ethical practices
- Individuals who expect overnight success without effort
- Anyone seeking guaranteed income
- Those unwilling to learn numbers, systems, and discipline

If you want fast money with no responsibility, this is not your path.

How to build a

SYSTEM

That

EARNS

For

YOU

SELECT. SOURCE. SELL EXISTING PRODUCTS &

GET PAID EVERY TWO WEEKS ON AMAZON

MAHIN ESHITA

www.ebusinessmastery.com

Paperback ISBN: 978-1-7640494-2-9
eBook ISBN: 978-1-7640494-3-6

First Edition 2026
Published by eBusiness Mastery
An imprint of Mx Lane Australia Pty Ltd

TABLE OF CONTENTS

CHAPTER 1

WHY SELL ON AMAZON

1.1 WHY SELL ON AMAZON?

Thank you for picking up this book. I'm Mahin — just a regular person with 10 + years' experience in online and (offline) businesses. Because I believe I should not work all day long on something I don't like, then come home in the evening tired and without the energy or focus to spend on myself or my loved ones.

When the weekend comes, I don't want to spend it recovering from a hard week, then cleaning, cooking, and doing other chores — and by the time I finish, it is Monday again.

Weeks, months, and years will go by, and one day I will think to myself:

Have I lived?

Have I loved?

Did I do something great that truly matters to me and my loved ones?

I'm afraid the answer would be NO.

Sorry — that life is not for me.

Instead, I always wanted to build something for myself that works for me all day long. And that something must support me financially so I can live on my own terms.

In that endeavor, I first started my online journey back in 2013 with my beautiful Shopify store. I knew nothing about building a business — online or digital marketing — at the time.

But I knew online was the way to build the life I wanted.

Without much experience, but with a little help from my better half, I built that Shopify store quickly and wanted to sell jewelry and scarves online. At the time, my hubby used to do passion photography, so I got him to take pictures and edit them to suit our product catalog needs.

We imported products from China and India and stocked them in our garage in Melbourne, Australia, where we live. We told all our friends and family about our exciting store.

Many of them bought.

But soon after launch, we exhausted all our contacts — and there was no more traffic.

So we decided to run paid ads using Facebook.

We did — but it turned out to be very expensive.

We were generating traffic and making some sales, but we were barely making any money.

We realized something important:

If there is no traffic to your Shopify store, there is no business. Period.

Not only did we need traffic, but we also had to:

- Create product listings
- Take pictures
- Edit photos
- Write descriptions

- Store inventory
- Pack products
- Ship orders
- Go to the post office
- Handle customer calls
- Manage complaints and returns
- And constantly struggle for traffic

I used to work more than 10–12 hours a day trying to make it work.

Honestly, it was not a fun journey at all.

I understand that some people have become successful with Shopify — but it was not for me. It took a huge toll on my personal life and made me anxious and stressed.

A few years into the Shopify business, I kept telling myself:

There must be a better way.

I remember, one day, my hubby San and I were driving around the Melbourne Cricket Ground (MCG), and he casually mentioned that he saw an ad on

Facebook about selling on Amazon. He attended the webinar, and apparently it would solve 70% of our problems — including traffic.

I said, "No way. It's just too good to be true."

So I attended the webinar myself.

Before I go any further, I want to say this:

Since 2013, we didn't just build a Shopify business. We also had a brick-and-mortar business — a coffee vending machine business across Melbourne — for about 2.5 years.

I can confidently say that building a business from scratch takes a lot of hard work, determination, consistency, and many mental, physical, and financial challenges.

When you go to YouTube and type "How to make money online," you'll find many gurus showing you the "laptop lifestyle."

You get motivated to start one.

But the truth is:

Online businesses are not "piece of cakes."

They are not any easier than traditional businesses.

They require products or services, systems, tools, marketing, sales, accounting, teams, compliance, taxes — and everything else you would need in a traditional business.

The laptop lifestyle is absolutely possible.

But not as quickly as it is often sold to you.

However, an online business frees you from being stuck in one physical location. And the opportunities are not capped the way they are in a brick-and-mortar business.

Now, going back to that webinar about selling on Amazon — I learned that Amazon FBA service provides features that allow aspiring entrepreneurs to start their online journey without worrying about many of the "must-have" elements required for any business (including online) to succeed.

After the webinar, I realized I didn't need to:

- Take pictures of my products and design listings on my own website

- Use my garage (or warehouse) to store, pack, or ship to customers

- Take customer calls, complaints, or handle returns

- Constantly promote my store

- And most importantly, look for traffic all day, every day — and be at the mercy of social media platforms to generate leads

And that's when I had an "Aha" moment.

I felt like I had stumbled upon a gold mine — something I could use to build that "something" that works for me all day long and supports my lifestyle so I can live on my own terms.

I started building my Amazon business in 2018.

I loved it so much that in my second year I became a six figure seller and grew from there.

Over the years, I have made hundreds of thousands of dollars and built a system that allows me to:

- Work from anywhere in the world while traveling

- Work on my own schedule

- Work with people I choose

- Scale to any level I want (the sky is the limit)

In this book, if you pay attention, I will show you how you can do that too.

1.2 A BUSINESS OWNER VS BUSINESS OPERATOR

Building, running, and scaling a business (online or traditional) requires you to wear a lot of hats at the same time — especially when you are starting out. You have to come up with the idea, create the product or service, constantly test and tweak it, improve it, package it into an offer, market it, sell it, deliver it, provide customer service — and finally, you may or may not see some profit (or even a loss), along with financial, physical, mental, and leadership challenges.

There are quite a few departments (i.e., product & services, quality assurance, sales, marketing, accounting, legal & taxes, team management, systems, customer service, logistics etc.) in your business (on a smaller scale too) that you will need to run all by yourself.

For any business, the first round from product to profit will be the hardest thing you do because you do not know the road ahead, and almost certainly you will face unanticipated roadblocks on the way to your first sale.

Guess what? Then you have to pay tax on your hard-earned profit.

Did you know that in the US, 81.9% of small businesses are operated by the owner only, with no paid employees (this number is 63.6% in Australia and 75% in the UK) according to recent statistics?

You might be scratching your head and thinking, what do these stats have to do with selling on Amazon?

Just bear with me for a second.

These stats mean that if you are a traditional or online business owner in the US, AU, UK, or similar regions, there is a very good chance you will fall into that 80% range — where you deal with everything in your business by yourself.

That approach makes you a self-employed "business operator," and that requires you to work IN the business 10–12 hours a day running those departments.

The truth is, in this model, you do not work for a boss or company — but you work for your own business as the only employee (often without decent pay while you are building it).

How can you live a life of freedom?

I believe the business must work for me — not the other way around.

That's why I want to highlight a concept in you:

From being a "Business Operator" to becoming a true "Business Owner."

A business owner is someone who owns a business that can run and make money without the owner.

You might think — how is this possible?

A true business owner replaces herself (or himself) with either systems, other people, or most commonly a combination of both.

Remember those departments of any business? Amazon FBA provides quite a few of the "DONE FOR YOU" departments so you do not have to worry about them.

That literally means less stress for you.

If you are starting out as an online entrepreneur and as a true business owner, you might not have the financial ability to hire people to work for you — but you can absolutely use Amazon FBA to build systems that take care of those departments (Infrastructure, Products, Dashboards, Payment handling, Warehouse, Packing & Shipping, Customer service etc.) in your business from the very beginning.

And we are not just talking about using services from any business — but from one of the best in the world: Amazon.

I wish I could tell you that you can build these systems from scratch very quickly, become financially free, live the laptop lifestyle, and all your dreams will come true (some Amazon gurus will tell you this) very quickly.

But yes — building systems on Amazon will take time, money, and effort from you (like anything worth having).

In the beginning, I said this book does not make promises or guarantee income or success. But I have done it, my students are doing it I can tell you if you have a burning desire and put in meaningful and consistent actions you will have a higher chance of success.

Initially, you will work 80%, and the system will work 20%.

After you build the end-to-end workflow on Amazon (i.e., 6–9 months to build solid, consistent income),

Then you will work 20%, and the system will work 80%.

Remember, as long as you comply with government regulations and Amazon policies, you can keep earning from these systems for a long time (there are sellers who have been on Amazon for 20+ years).

That's how you become an almost true business owner using Amazon FBA systems — free up your time and live your life the way you want.

Decision for you would be to be a true business owner.

1.3 SEVEN MYTHS ABOUT AMAZON

I want to put your mind at ease by addressing the 7 most common myths about Amazon.

Myth 1 (Money Block): I need thousands of dollars to start on Amazon.

Truth: You can start with $500–$700 with most authentic suppliers. Test the waters first, then slowly build to the next level.

Myth 2 (Time Block): I need 4–6 hours a day to build my Amazon business.

Truth: Most beginners gain traction with 10–15 hours a week and can become successful.

Myth 3 (False Belief): Amazon is saturated — I'm too late.

Truth: Saturation happens when you sell a seasonal or hyped product that too many people are selling. I will show you how to avoid them.

Myth 4 (False Belief): I'm not technical — it's too complex.

Truth: If you know how to use Google, ChatGPT, Excel, and a few basic tools, you can do this. My hubby joked the other day that even my grandma could do it ☺

Myth 5 (False Belief): I don't know how to sell or pay for ads to make money.

Truth: I teach you how to find products that are already selling organically, so you do not need push selling on platforms like Facebook, Google, or Instagram. You can use Amazon ads if you want — but it's optional.

Myth 6 (False Belief): Suppliers are hard to work with.

Truth: People struggle when they approach the wrong suppliers (especially at the beginning). I will show you how to filter and build gradually.

Myth 7 (False Belief): I don't know how to send traffic to my Amazon products.

Truth: You will use Amazon's own traffic. You do not need to send traffic from other platforms because Amazon already has over 255 million active customers.

If you notice, all those false beliefs sound like complaints or excuses.

Anything worth doing or having will come with challenges — including building business systems on Amazon.

Be careful what you feed your mind with. If you focus on finding problems on Amazon (or any business), you will certainly find them.

But if you focus on finding solutions to the challenges you will undoubtedly face — you will find those too.

1.4 YOUR OPPORTUNITY

Everyday people like you and me have been selling on Amazon since the year 2000. In a recent email from Amazon, it was stated that in the last 25 years (2000–2025), selling partners (Amazon third-party sellers) generated more than $2.5 trillion.

Can you believe that?

In 2025, Amazon's revenue was estimated at $830 billion (Marketplace Pulse research). Of that, approximately $525 billion was generated by Amazon selling partners — accounting for more than 60% of Amazon's total revenue.

If you are not yet selling on Amazon, you are potentially missing out on a massive opportunity to build and grow your business on this platform and create the life you want.

1.5 HOW BIG CAN YOU GO ON AMAZON?

When I first started on Amazon in 2018, my goal was to make a side income with minimal effort. That's exactly why I chose Amazon — as I said earlier, I like systems that work for me 24/7.

Some of my students ask:

"I've been selling on Amazon for a while and consistently making side income — but how big can I go?"

That's an excellent question.

According to Marketplace Pulse research, 235 Amazon sellers are generating annual revenue of $100M+ at the time of this writing.

So yes — the sky is the limit ☺

1.6 WHY THE WHOLESALE MODEL?

There are many different business models within Amazon. If you are just starting out, start with the wholesale model.

I have outlined six main reasons:

- **Reason 1** (Established Demand & Trust): You sell products that Amazon customers already trust, and you can see the demand through existing listings.

- **Reason 2** (Data Is Visible Before You Risk Money): Historical data, hundreds of metrics, and competition levels are visible for you to analyze and make informed decisions based on real data — not emotion.

- **Reason 3** (No Branding or Marketing Genius Required): A private label beginner must learn product design, photography, keywords, copywriting, PPC, ranking, and more — which may (or will) feel overwhelming. The wholesale model skips most of that.

- **Reason 4** (Faster Sales): Everything about the product already exists. When your inventory arrives at Amazon, you plug into the product's organic selling rhythm with proper pricing and inventory levels — and you can start selling by adjusting a few parameters.

- **Reason 5** (Avoid Unsold Inventory): If a private label launch fails (which happens often because there is no established demand), you are stuck with inventory. In wholesale, if your product research is solid, this risk is significantly lower.

- **Reason 6** (Scale Predictably): After a few inventory cycles, you understand how the product behaves, which allows you to predict and orchestrate sales more accurately for future months or years.

Do not get trapped in thousands of non-value-adding tasks.

For example, you are analyzing an existing listing and thinking the picture quality could be better. That does not add value in the wholesale model — because that "unattractive" picture is already selling.

Especially when you are just beginning and want everything to be perfect before taking action — it will slow you down.

1.7 THREE SECRETS YOU NEED TO KNOW

I hope I have given you a glimpse of what's possible on Amazon and the opportunity you have to build, run, and grow your business on it.

I believe you are already convinced and excited ☺

From this point forward, I will go straight to the point in most sections of this book.

Here are the 3 secrets behind the SSS (Select → Source → Sell) system — even if you start from zero:

- **Secret #1** – How to select products that are already selling (and you potentially can analyze them in minutes).

- **Secret #2** – How to source them from authentic suppliers — even if you are starting with a low budget and zero experience.

- **Secret #3** – How to set up an automatic sales system that sells your inventory day after day (so you don't get stuck) — without ads.

That's all you need to master for your freedom income on Amazon.

See you in the next chapter ☺

CHAPTER 2

SETUP AND GO LIVE ON AMAZON

2.1 SELL AS A BUSINESS (NOT PERSONAL)

When you are starting out, it may be tempting to use a personal account to sell on Amazon rather than a professional business account.

As I mentioned before, this book is not about getting rich quickly by selling seasonal or hyped products just to make some money. If you are serious about building solid and consistent income on Amazon, this is your book.

And for that reason, please do not use a personal account to sell on Amazon.

There are many reasons why you should have a professional business account, but I want to give you a simple example to make this point clear.

At the time of this writing, Amazon charges $0.99 per unit sold on a personal account, on top of all other fees. Now think about this — if you sell 1,000 units in a month, you will pay $990 to Amazon from your profit. If you sell 2,000 units, you will pay $1,980.

This is not sustainable and eats into your profit on every single unit you sell.

Start with a professional account. It is about $39.99 per month, gives you unlimited monthly units, and provides many more features that benefit your long-term Amazon business.

2.2 CHOOSE YOUR MARKETPLACE

Start with Amazon.com in the US. At the time of this writing, it has about 255 million active customers and is by far the largest Amazon marketplace. The closest are

Germany and the UK, with about 15 million active customers each.

The US marketplace has the highest amount of organic traffic compared to other countries.

If you are based outside the US, you can still build your business in the US and sell on Amazon.com as a native US business or a foreign entity (for example, if your business is registered in the UK or Australia).

2.3 PREPARATION (ONCE OFF)

When you sell as a business, you want to prepare your business documents first before opening your Amazon professional account.

1. If you do not have a business yet, it is relatively easy to form an LLC (Limited Liability Company) using an agent in any US state you prefer. For example, if you live in Florida, you can find an agent online (just Google "form an LLC in the US"), pay a few hundred dollars plus the state fee, and they will handle the paperwork and lodge it with the state. Usually, within 5–7 business days, your business will be formed.

2. Get the EIN (Employer Identification Number) for your business. This is usually done by the agent. In the US, it takes a few days. If you are outside the US, it may take a few weeks.

3. Once your business is formed and you have your EIN, you have the main requirements to open the Amazon.com professional selling account under your business name.

4. Go to https://sellercentral.amazon.com/, click "Sign Up," follow the prompts, provide your business and personal details as requested, and verify your identity. This process typically takes 10–15 minutes. Sometimes Amazon may take 24–48 hours to verify your identity. Once completed, they will email you confirming that you are ready to list your first product.

If you encounter any issues during or after account setup, you can log in to Amazon Seller Central and contact Amazon Support via chat or raise a case with them. They will help you rectify anything that needs fixing.

Remember, this sign-up process is done only once. Once your professional business account is active, you are ready to go.

2.4 AMAZON ACCOUNT HEALTH CHECK

Once your Amazon account is set up, log in and check if there are any alerts or action items that need your attention before doing anything else. You want to make sure your account is in good health before listing your first product.

At minimum, ensure the following:

- Your business information and address match your legal documents

- Your ID verification is complete and no action is required

- Your tax interview questions are answered and completed with a green tick

- You have provided a valid credit/debit card so Amazon can charge you

- You have provided a valid bank account so Amazon can pay you

- Your Account Health page shows green, with no red or yellow alerts

- Two-step verification is ON
- Go to Performance → Notifications and ensure no action is pending

If you see any alert or pending action and are unsure what it means, contact Amazon Support via chat or raise a case. They will guide you.

Next is a small mindset tip.

You are the business owner, and this business is your baby. There may be unexpected issues inside or outside Amazon that are not covered in this book (or any other book). As a business owner, address issues with confidence and good faith. Do the right thing — even if it feels daunting at first. This mindset will pay off in the long run.

Build this with a long-term vision, and do not let small obstacles stop you.

Once you reach this point — Congratulations! You now have an active Amazon.com account and are ready to look for products and suppliers.

In the next chapter, I will show you how to find your first product and list it on Amazon.

CHAPTER 3

SELECT PRODUCTS

3.1 SEVEN THINGS YOU WANT TO KNOW ABOUT AMAZON

In our SSS (SELECT, SOURCE, SELL) System, we only sell products that are already selling on Amazon, so there is demand and trust from customers that we can utilize to our benefit.

But there are millions of products to choose from.

How do you know which ones will make you consistent money?

If you try to choose from such a large pool with so many different business models on Amazon, you will easily get overwhelmed and fail to take meaningful action.

That's why I have outlined 7 things for you so you can filter out the rest:

- Only choose products that you can reorder over and over again (no seasonal or hyped products).

- Source your products from authorized and authentic suppliers only.

- Check for stable sales velocity (i.e., X units/month on average) over a long period.

- Ensure the product is profitable after all costs.

- Avoid products that are overcrowded with other sellers.

- Go for simple items that are easy to pack, ship, and return (even though you are using Amazon FBA).

- Avoid monopolized listings.

All seven conditions must be met when selecting products for this model.

3.2 AMAZON TERMINOLOGIES

When dealing with products, suppliers, or Amazon, there are many terms you will come across. If you are just beginning your journey, you might think, "I have no idea what that means." But you can always find out using ChatGPT or other tools.

You do not need to memorize all of them. There are only a few that you will see repeatedly, and you will automatically remember them after a few rounds.

Here are the key ones you will need from day one:

- **ASIN – Amazon Standard Identification Number:** This is an Amazon-specific term used to uniquely identify a product within their ecosystem. When you contact support about a product, this is the first thing they will ask for.

- **FBA – Fulfilled by Amazon:** This is the service we use in this model, where Amazon stores, packs, ships your products, and provides customer service.

- **FBM – Fulfilled by Merchant:** When you see FBM on a listing, it means the seller handles storage, packing, shipping, and customer service themselves.

- **Buy Box:** This is the main "Add to Cart" button on any Amazon product listing. When a customer clicks that button, Amazon assigns a seller (like you) to fulfill that sale — provided you are priced competitively and have sufficient inventory and other factors. I will explain this further later.

- **UPC – Universal Product Code:** This is similar to ASIN but universal, meaning it is recognized outside Amazon across vendors, distributors, and manufacturers. Suppliers typically do not understand ASINs, so you will use UPC when referring to a product with them and with their own item number.

- **BSR – Best Seller Rank:** Every product on Amazon has a rank that changes frequently. It indicates how well the product is selling within its category.

- **ROI – Return on Investment:** When calculating profit, you also need to understand how much money you must invest to make that profit — that is your ROI.

Don't stress about memorizing everything. As you work on your Amazon business, you will naturally become familiar with these terms.

3.3 FIVE STEPS TO VALIDATE ANY PRODUCT

This is where you want to pay full attention. In fact, I suggest you memorize this as soon as possible.

Every product you consider selling must answer these 5 questions:

Question 1 (Ensure Demand):

How many units are sold on Amazon per month?

Because we only sell existing products, not all products sell consistently. You want to select products that already have proven demand.

Question 2 (Check Competition):

How many other sellers are selling this product?

A product may have strong demand (like a hyped product), but if too many sellers are offering the same product, you will experience saturation. You want to avoid overcrowded listings.

Question 3 (Check Your Portion):

How many units will you realistically sell per month?

If you are satisfied with demand and competition (Q1 and Q2), you must estimate your portion of total monthly sales so you can predict your future revenue and profit.

Question 4 (Check Profit):

How much profit will you make per unit?

Even if your portion looks good, you must ensure the product is profitable after all costs.

Question 5 (Check ROI):

What is the ROI on this product?

You must understand how much capital is required to generate the expected profit. For example, if you make $5 profit per unit, you might need to invest $12 to purchase that unit from the supplier and other fees.

These five questions are the foundation of product selection. They ensure demand, velocity, profitability, competition control, and proper capital allocation — before you invest any money.

3.4 HOW DO YOU VALIDATE THESE 5 STEPS?

You can use several software tools to validate these five questions. At the time of this writing, multiple tools are available on the market.

Before discussing tools, I want to highlight a critical aspect of product research. There are two methods to find profitable existing products on Amazon:

Method 1: Product → Supplier

In this method, you find a product on Amazon first, then identify the brand and supplier. You validate it using the five steps at least (and additional checks, more later). Once satisfied, you place the order and ship inventory to Amazon warehouses.

For this method, you can use tools such as Helium10, Jungle Scout, Keepa, and similar software. You can choose a niche (e.g., Toys), run searches, and analyze existing selling products.

Method 2: Supplier → Product

In this method, you open an account with a supplier or distributor first. For example, you decide to sell Disney toys. You find authorized distributors, open an account, obtain their catalog (Excel, CSV, or PDF), and analyze the products for profitability.

For this method, you can use tools like Analyzer.Tools, or similar tools. They allow you to upload supplier catalogs and quickly analyze hundreds or thousands of SKUs.

In both methods, the objective remains the same: validate the product using the five steps first, then apply additional checks to minimize risk and increase confidence.

3.5 HOW TO TEST PRODUCTS WITHOUT WASTING MONEY?

Once you have selected one or multiple products using either method, the next step is testing.

Remember, the goal is to find products that can become long-term "soldiers" — products that sustain profitability over multiple rounds and eventually reduce your need to constantly search for new items.

Here are 5 things to focus on when testing:

1. Buy small quantities. When testing, order only the minimum required (e.g., 20 units) to reduce risk.

2. Use tool data, not emotion. Validate the product thoroughly before placing any order.

3. Avoid restricted brands. Tools will indicate if a product has brand restrictions. As you grow, you can apply for gated brands later.

4. Monitor performance. After selling your initial batch, evaluate sales velocity and profitability.

5. Only reorder if proven. Do not scale products that fail to meet your performance expectations.

3.6 QUICK CONSISTENT INCOME TIP

For consistent income, your products must be replenishable.

That means constant demand on Amazon and reliable supply from your distributor. Avoid seasonal items (e.g., back-to-school supplies) and short-term hyped products.

Focus on essential, everyday products that people need regularly (e.g., kitchen gadgets, hand towels, household essentials).

3.7 BASIC PRODUCT RESEARCH CHECKLIST

Before finishing this chapter, here is a basic checklist you can use for every product you evaluate:

Check Demand and Stability

☐ At least 180-day trend confirms no sharp drop

☐ No heavy seasonal spikes (unless planned)

☐ Sales rank history stable (Keepa)

☐ No sudden price collapses in past 6–12 months

☐ Average sales rank not over 170k

Check Competition

☐ Number of FBA sellers (check over at least 180 days)

☐ Is Amazon on the listing? (Make sure Amazon is not selling it)

☐ Seller ratings — are competitors weak or strong?

Check Profitability

☐ Average selling price in last 180 days

☐ Profitable even at historical low price

☐ Acceptable profit margin

☐ Shipping weight/FBA fees reasonable

☐ Prep/labeling/shipping costs included (usually $1–$2.50 per unit in Kitchen category)

Check Consistent Demand and Supply

☐ Brand/supplier has history (not brand-new)

☐ Can provide authentic invoice for Amazon

☐ Regular restocking possible

☐ Reviews accumulated over years

☐ Not hazmat or restricted

The main idea is simple:

- Boring products that sell every day.

- Low competition.

- Decent demand.

Once you secure some of these and complete a few successful rounds, they can generate consistent income for years.

3.8 LIST YOUR PRODUCT ON AMAZON FIRST

Once you select a product, the first thing you should do is try listing it on Amazon.

Remember, you are not creating a new listing. You are adding yourself to an existing listing and offering inventory.

Listing first gives you clarity:

- Is the product gated?

- Does it require brand approval?

- Are there category restrictions?

- Are there hazmat flags?

- Is it restricted?

If you cannot add it to inventory, what is the point of opening a supplier account?

Listing first removes blind risk.

Imagine opening 10 supplier accounts for products you later cannot list — that is wasted time.

Listing first means:

Only serious SKUs move forward.

Data → Listing → Validation → Supplier → Purchase.

Not:

Excitement → Supplier → Inventory → Panic.

3.9 HOW TO ACTUALLY LIST THE PRODUCT

Log in to Seller Central → Inventory → Add a product → Search by ASIN/UPC → Click "Sell this product."

You will see one of two options:

Option 1: "Apply to sell"

This means the product is gated. You will need approval and a paid authentic invoice from a legitimate supplier. Amazon typically reviews approval within 1–2 days.

Option 2: "You are approved to sell"

This means your account is eligible to sell the product immediately, sometimes it may not say that you are approved, it will go straight to the next page.

If you are approved:

- Enter your SKU (internal name)

- Set condition to New

- Choose Fulfillment Method (FBA)

- Set your price (you can change this later)

Amazon will show detailed FBA fees. These are deducted after each sale (not paid upfront), allowing you to calculate your projected profit before investing.

You can save the listing without creating a shipment yet. First, confirm details with the supplier to ensure margins are accurate.

Correct sequence:

1. Product selected

2. Add ASIN to Seller Central

3. Confirm no restrictions

4. Confirm fees

5. Confirm Buy Box viability

6. THEN contact supplier

This is the safest approach when starting out.

For gated products (Option 1):

Click "Apply to sell." Amazon will request a paid invoice for a specific minimum quantity (e.g., 20 units). You must purchase inventory, obtain the invoice, and submit it for approval. Once approved, you proceed with shipment.

After approval, you send products directly to Amazon warehouses or via a prep center (covered later).

CHAPTER 4

SOURCE

In the previous chapter, we talked about how to select existing products that already sell on Amazon for consistent income.

That is probably the most important skill you will develop to build, run, and grow your business on Amazon — and it will help you create the life you want using the "system."

In this chapter, we focus on where and how to source those products.

We source from inside the US from US based suppliers. This model removes the complexities of handling customs etc.

4.1 TYPES OF SUPPLIERS

Not all suppliers are the same. Generally, there are four types of companies you can source your products from.

Manufacturers

As the name suggests, they own the factories and sometimes have the highest authority over the product. They may own the brand and control the market and supply chain in many ways.

Pros: Lowest cost per unit, most legitimate source

Cons: Often high MOQ (minimum order quantity) and longer lead times

Your strategy:

If you are just starting out, it may be difficult to test products directly from manufacturers because the MOQ is high. However, if you are already selling that brand through distributors, it is worth checking with the manufacturer directly — it may increase your margins.

Distributors / Wholesalers

These are authorized distributors from the brand and/or manufacturer. They can be located anywhere in the country (e.g., US) or even overseas.

For example, a brand in Italy may have distributors in the US. You can source products from the US distributor. Usually, authorized distributors are listed publicly on the brand's website.

Pros: Easier access to multiple brands with valid invoices

Cons: Slightly higher prices (obviously) and sometimes brand limitations

Your strategy:

In the US, these are typically the suppliers you want to work with. You can source from outside the US, but you will need to deal with customs and it may be harder to verify legitimacy.

Retailers / Online Stores

These are public retailers (e.g., Walmart, Target, etc.) where you can purchase known brands and resell on Amazon (at the time of this writing).

Pros: Easy to start, lower MOQ, quick sourcing, occasional discounted opportunities

Cons: Not scalable or sustainable, Amazon may not accept retail receipts, potential IP risks

Your strategy:

If you are serious about building a solid business, this sourcing method is not sustainable. You will constantly chase discounts and it will not free up your time. I do not recommend this approach.

Brands (Direct Account)

This means opening an account directly with the brand.

Pros: Best pricing, strongest invoice credibility, stronger long-term relationship

Cons: Harder approval for new sellers, slower communication, stricter policies

Your strategy:

Once you have built a portfolio of brands, reach out for direct accounts. If you are brand new, start with distributors first and build your track record.

For example, if you already sell Adidas through an authorized distributor, it may be easier to get approved with Nike. If you sell neither, approval will be much harder.

Think of it like a credit score — once you build credibility, more doors open.

4.2 GOOD SUPPLIERS ARE THE PILLARS OF YOUR BUSINESS

Think of your house — it is built on pillars. If the pillars are weak, the house becomes vulnerable.

Your Amazon business is the same. Authentic suppliers are the pillars of your business.

If your product supply gets interrupted, so does your revenue.

When I started in 2018, I had only two suppliers. The following year, one of them went out of stock on five of my highest-revenue products. My overall revenue dropped by about 40%.

I learned the hard way — you want at least five suppliers generating revenue so that if one supplier stops, you only take a 20% hit.

On the other hand, my second supplier supported about 60% of my revenue — even during COVID (2019–2021). They were impacted, but not severely.

Mainly because of two reasons:

First, I was selling boring but essential daily products. Even during COVID, people cut expenses — but they still bought essentials like paper towels and hand wash.

Second, that supplier was legitimate — was in business for over 40 years with strong supply chain control. I had built a strong relationship with them.

Bottom line: The more suppliers and products you have, the stronger your business becomes.

4.3 WHERE DO YOU FIND THOSE SUPPLIERS?

There are at least four ways to find legitimate suppliers.

Brand Website

If you want to sell a specific brand, go to the brand's official website and look for a wholesale or authorized distributor link.

You can also search:

"Brand name + wholesale"

or consult ChatGPT for distributor information.

Wholesale Directories

You can use free and paid directories to find supplier contact details.

Examples (no affiliation, no guarantees):

- worldwidebrands.com (paid)

- salehoo.com (free and paid)

- thomasnet.com (free and paid)

These directories are entry points. You still need to contact suppliers using proper business credentials and open an account professionally.

Avoid suppliers that pose scam risks.

Trade Shows & Exhibitions

You can attend trade shows in person or review exhibitor lists.

Examples:

- ASD Market Week – Las Vegas
- OFFPRICE Show – Las Vegas
- PPAI Expo – Las Vegas
- Global Pet Expo – Florida

Thousands of suppliers attend these events and are often open to new accounts.

Google & AI Search

Use search queries such as:

"Wholesale distributor + [Brand name]"

"Authorized [Brand Name] distributor in the US"

This helps you locate websites and contact details quickly.

4.4 HOW TO APPROACH A DISTRIBUTOR OR SUPPLIER

Let me be direct.

Not all suppliers will open accounts for you.

Many will not reply. Some will say no.

The mindset is: it is not about you or your business.

I will repeat that.

It is not about you or your business.

Many beginners make the following mistakes and do not get approved,

Mistake 1 (Positioning)

Using Gmail, no website, no reseller certificate, no phone number, no professional email signature.

Supplier assumption: You are flipping products short-term.

Solution:

Use a proper domain email, simple website, reseller certificate, business phone, and professional signature.

Mistake 2 (Purchase Power)

Saying, "I want to order 5 units."

Supplier thinks: Is this worth onboarding?

Solution:

Respect MOQ. Communicate projected volume for future orders.

Mistake 3 (Wrong Supplier)

Some suppliers sell directly on Amazon and prohibit resellers.

Solution:

Move on.

Mistake 4 (No Follow-Up)

Beginners send one email and wait forever.

Suppliers receive hundreds (sometimes thousands) of emails daily. Yours may land in spam.

Solution:

Day 1 – Initial email

Day 3 – Follow-up email

Day 5 – First call

Day 7 – Second call

Day 10 – Third call

No response after multiple attempts? Move on.

Mistake 5 (Not Understanding the Numbers Game)

Many beginners contact 10–20 suppliers and quit.

Account opening is a numbers game.

If 3 say yes out of 50 serious attempts — that is success.

You do not need hundreds of suppliers.

Start with 2–3 (first 3–6 months).

Build to 5–7 (6–12 months).

Scale to 10–15 (1–2 years).

Set expectations properly and you reduce disappointment.

4.5 WHAT DO YOU WRITE IN EMAILS?

Do not write essays.

Keep emails short, professional, and specific.

Sample Email

Email 1 (initial contact sample)

Dear [Supplier Name / Sales Team],

My name is [Name] from [Company Name], a registered U.S. wholesale retail business.

We are expanding our supplier network and are interested in opening a wholesale account with your company. We focus on long-term partnerships and consistent reorders.

Please advise on the account application process. I am happy to provide our resale certificate and any required documentation.

Thank you for your time, and I look forward to your response.

Kind regards,

[Full Name]
[Company Name]
[Website]
[Phone Number]

Email 2 (Follow up after 3 – 4 days)

Dear [Supplier Name / Sales Team],

I wanted to briefly follow up on my previous email regarding opening a wholesale account with your company.

We are actively onboarding new supplier relationships and remain very interested in reviewing your product catalog and wholesale terms.

Please let me know if there is a specific application form or additional documentation required from our side.

Thank you for your time, and I look forward to your response.

Kind regards,

[Full Name]
[Company Name]
[Website]
[Phone Number]

Sample Phone Script with a sales representative:

The goal of the first call is not approval. It is:

- introduce yourself
- sound professional
- confirm process
- open a relationship
- gather qualification info
- Keep it confident, calm and short.

Step 1 – Opening

Hi, this is [Your Name] from [Company Name].

I'm calling regarding opening a wholesale account and wanted to briefly introduce our business.

Pause.

Let them respond.

Step 2 – Establish Professional Positioning

We're a registered U.S. wholesale retail business and currently expanding our supplier partnerships this quarter.

I wanted to understand your process for onboarding new accounts.

Keep it neutral.

Do NOT jump into Amazon yet.

Step 3 – Qualification Question

Are you currently accepting new wholesale partners?

Let them answer.

If YES:

That's great. What documentation or application steps are required on our end?

If MAYBE / NOT SURE:

No problem. Could you guide me on what you typically look for when approving new accounts?

If NO:

I understand. May I ask what qualifications are usually required for consideration in the future?

Step 4 – If Amazon Comes Up

If they ask:

"Do you sell on Amazon?"

Respond calmly:

We operate across multiple retail channels and strictly follow brand pricing and compliance guidelines.

Our focus is long-term, responsible distribution in multiple channels including Amazon.

Short. Confident. No defensiveness.

Step 5 – Close Professionally

I appreciate your time.

I'll send over our resale certificate and company details shortly.

Thank you for guiding me through the next steps.

Tips to remember during the call.

- Slow pace
- Smile while speaking

- Stand while calling (improves voice confidence)

- Never sound desperate

- Never oversell

What NOT To Say

"I just started selling on Amazon."

"Can I get invoices for ungating?"

"What's your MOQ? I want something small."

"Do you allow Amazon sellers?" (too blunt)

4.6 WHAT IS A RESELLER PERMIT?

A reseller permit (resale certificate or sales tax permit) is issued by a US state. It allows your business to purchase inventory tax-free because it is for resale — not personal use.

Suppliers require it because it proves:

- You are a registered business

- You are authorized to buy tax-exempt

- You are not a retail customer

If your business has nexus in multiple states (inventory stored, employees, office, etc.), you may need permits in those states.

Always apply through official state websites (.gov).

Important:

This is a legal tax document. You must maintain proper records.

4.7 HOW TO FILTER SUPPLIERS

The question is, how do you identify the legit and authentic suppliers so you do not waste time on the others (not so legit) suppliers.

That's why I have created a simple checklist you can follow before approaching the suppliers for accounts, this will save you a lot of time.

Look for some of these things when checking an authentic supplier: (this is most critical for Amazon and save your investment)

- Professional website (not Shopify template reselling random brands)

- Business domain email (not Gmail/Yahoo)

- Physical address listed

- Phone number clearly displayed

- About Us page with history

- Clear wholesale or distributor language

- Verify business license upon approval

- Listed as "authorized distributor" on brand website

- Requests resale certificate

- Requires account approval

- Requires login for pricing

- Provides line sheet or catalog after approval

- Realistic wholesale margins (i.e., 8% - 25% range depending on category)

- MOQ requirements reasonable

- Professional sales rep

- Clear onboarding steps

- Account application form

- Credit terms discussion

- Recognizable brands

- UPCs match official products

- Can provide proper wholesale invoice
- Industry references
- Trade show participation
- Attend ASD, Global Pet Expo, Toy Fair, etc.
- Appear in Thomasnet
- Appear in industry directories
- Exhibit at wholesale expos
- Has been in business for a while (e.g., 8+ years)

Run away from the suppliers with:

- No minimum order
- Huge discounts on all brands
- Retail-style checkout cart without login
- No company history
- They sell to anyone instantly with no paperwork.
- 70% off major brands
- Pricing identical to Amazon retail price
- Too good to be true margins
- Only WhatsApp contact
- No real company rep

- Too excited to work with you
- No invoice provided
- Generic invoice template
- Cash only
- No digital footprint

If 2 – 3 things from this 'run away' list become true for any supplier run away fast.

The bottom line is,

Real wholesalers:

- Protect brands
- Screen retailers
- Want long-term partners
- Move slower
- Require paperwork

Fake wholesalers:

- Approve instantly
- Offer huge discounts
- Don't verify you

- Don't care about brand protection

- If it's easy to get approved, question it.

I just wanted to say, build long term relationships with authentic suppliers it would be worth it.

CHAPTER 5

SELL

This is the part where the magic happens 

You can literally sleep — or do whatever you want — while your inventory gets sold on Amazon.

But before we get into this exciting part of your business, I want to talk about two more things that are directly related to selling.

5.1 WHAT ARE PREP CENTERS AND WHY DO YOU NEED THEM?

Once you have chosen the supplier and the products, you will pay for the inventory and the supplier will ship your products to your nominated location.

Because you are running an Amazon business, your inventory must be shipped to Amazon warehouses. Amazon will then receive the units, link them to your seller account, and store them in one or multiple fulfillment centers. (Amazon decides how inventory is distributed. You have no control over this — and you do not need to. Their algorithm knows where demand is.)

There are two basic requirements before inventory reaches Amazon:

1. Preparing and labeling each unit according to Amazon's warehouse standards (for example, poly bags, suffocation warnings, barcode labels, etc.) for most items.

2. Shipping the prepared inventory to Amazon warehouses using a carrier (UPS, FedEx, etc.)

You might be thinking:

How am I going to do this?

It's simple.

Prepping and labeling must be done — but who does it?

Some suppliers offer prep and labeling services. If they do, you can pay for that service (for example, $0.30 per unit) when placing your order. After prep is complete, they ship directly to Amazon.

If your supplier does not offer prep/label services, you will need a third-party warehouse. In this industry, that is called a **Prep Center**.

In that case:

Supplier → ships to Prep Center

Prep Center preps and labels

Prep Center → ships to Amazon

Once Amazon receives your inventory, they check it in and make it live for sale.

That is why you need a prep center account for your business.

If your prep center is located in a different state (for example, New York), you may need a reseller permit for that state if inventory is stored there.

To find one, simply search:

"Amazon FBA Prep Center + [Your State]"

Call them. Ask questions. Open account. Build a relationship.

Most prep centers are much easier to open accounts with than suppliers. Some may have minimum monthly volume requirements. Be transparent about your growth plans.

5.2 CREATING SHIPMENTS

Many prep centers will request limited access to your Seller Central account. They can integrate with Amazon and create shipments on your behalf.

If your supplier ships directly to Amazon, they may ask you for shipping labels. In that case, you must create the shipment inside Seller Central.

Go to: Inventory → Manage All Inventory → Send/Replenish Inventory

Each shipment is slightly different. Amazon Seller University has step-by-step videos — I recommend watching them once. After that, it takes only a few minutes each time.

Do not overthink this part. It becomes routine quickly.

5.3 UNDERSTAND BUY BOX AND AUTOMATED SELLING WHILE YOU SLEEP

When customers click "Add to Cart" on Amazon, they usually buy from the seller who holds the **Buy Box** at that time of purchase.

If multiple sellers offer the same product, Amazon rotates the Buy Box between eligible sellers based on:

- Price

- Inventory levels

- Shipping speed (FBA helps significantly)

- Seller performance

- Account health

Let's imagine Product A has four sellers — three experienced sellers and you as a new seller.

If you price responsibly and use FBA, Amazon may rotate the Buy Box among all qualified sellers. It is not always the lowest price that wins — it is the best overall combination of price and performance.

This is where a **repricer** becomes powerful.

A repricer is a software that automatically adjusts your price within limits you set. If another seller lowers price slightly, your repricer can respond within seconds. If competitors go out of stock, your price can increase strategically.

Remember, other sellers also have repricers, if they are configured correctly, a healthy rotation happens between all the sellers on that product all day every day.

Instead of manually checking listings all day, your system works in the background.

The result?

You don't create your own product.

You don't need heavy marketing.

You don't chase customers.

You plug into an existing marketplace.

When your account is healthy, your inventory is in stock, and your repricer is configured correctly, you are participating in a live 24/7 marketplace.

Sales can happen while you are working, traveling, or sleeping.

That is the power of understanding the Buy Box within the Amazon FBA system.

5.4 DO YOU NEED PAID ADS?

Yes, you can have paid ads on Amazon for your products, but that's not mandatory for this model that I'm talking about.

Paid ads are very useful (in fact needed) for Private Label products, where you launch your own product, create the Amazon listing.

So, when people search for a pillow case for example and you have your own branded pillow case listed and you are excited to be found on Amazon

But your listing does not come up and customers will not be able to find your listing and you will not make any sale.

Unless, you pay Amazon to show your product to customers using paid ads.

That's where paid ads are very useful.

For our model, remember the product research we did when we selected our products that are already selling?

Our research model is such that we only sell the products that are already coming on the top results on Amazon when customers search for it (i.e., Sales rank < 170k).

As I said earlier, sales rank of a product determines how well the product is selling on Amazon. That's why our product research has this filter to have (generally) the average sales ranks below <170k that ensures sales velocity and demand.

Honestly, when I first started selling on Amazon on my second year I did 6 figures <u>without</u> any paid ads.

In fact I did not use paid ads until my 3rd year.

So, you can imagine, you can do that too ☺

That's why I'm not talking about listing optimization (which I didn't do either because most listings are already optimized) or keywords improvements or paid ads in this book.

But do they help your sales in this wholesale model?

Yes but it would also help your competitors as they are selling from the same listing ☺

And yes, if you want to learn more about paid ads or keywords or listing optimization please check our website for more at www.ebusinessmastery.com

---

5.5 THE SYSTEM WORKS 80% AND YOU WORK 20%

Remember in Chapter 1 I mentioned this concept. Once you:

- Set up your business (once-off)
- Select replenishable products with demand
- Source from authentic suppliers
- Build supplier relationships
- Set up your prep center
- Configure listings and repricer correctly
- Maintain strong account health

And after you complete multiple selling cycles and receive consistent Amazon payouts every two weeks —

That is called consistency.

At this stage, the system works 80% and you work 20%.

What remains for you?

Business-as-usual tasks:

- Check sales and profit
- Monitor alerts
- Review inventory levels
- Adjust repricer if needed
- Reorder inventory
- Resolve occasional issues

How long does that take?

Often around one hour per day.

Yes, unexpected issues can arise — but if you follow policies and operate correctly, they are manageable and infrequent.

Compare that to working 9–5 or being a business operator working 10–12 hours per day.

This model gives your time back.

Imagine your Monday mornings without having to catch the train for work.

Your Wednesday afternoons stressing about picking your kids from school.

Your Thursday lunch break with your annoying boss.

None of them are needed.

Every day of the week is yours.

You choose, whatever you want to do.

CHAPTER 6

OPTIMIZE & SCALE

6.1 AMAZON PAYS EVERY TWO WEEKS

At this point, I believe you would have already sold a few products and may have completed a few rounds of the same products.

That means you are becoming consistent in selling good, authentic ASINs sourced from legitimate suppliers.

Amazon pays you every two weeks to your nominated deposit method (for example, your bank account).

Every Amazon payout has two components:

1. Your COGS (Cost of Goods Sold)

2. Your Gross Profit

Your job is to be disciplined.

When Amazon pays you, immediately separate:

- The COGS amount from the profit amount

COGS generally includes:

- Product cost paid to supplier

- Prep/label costs

- Shipping costs

(Note: FBA fees are already deducted before Amazon pays you, so you do not need to manually subtract them.)

Pay back your COGS to the card you used to purchase inventory (credit card or debit card). This frees up your credit limit and keeps your inventory cycle rotating.

Then separate your profit and ideally transfer it into a separate account (for example, a "Profit Account").

This allows you to clearly see how much you are truly making.

If you want to grow without injecting new money from your pocket, reinvesting profit is a smart strategy.

But always separate it first.

Visibility creates discipline.

6.2 HOW DO YOU SEPARATE COGS FROM PROFIT?

The general rule:

Amazon Pay = COGS + Profit

During a settlement period (two weeks), let's say you sold:

- 10 units of Product A

- 20 units of Product B

You can get this data from Reports in Seller Central.

Step1: Now calculate what you actually paid per unit:

- COGS A = Product price + prep/label + shipping

Step2: Then multiply by the number of units sold in that settlement period for each product and calculate total COGS.

- (COGS A X 10) + (COGS B X 20) = TOTAL COGS (Pay this back to your card)

Step3: Calculate Gross Profit

- Gross Profit = Amazon's Pay − TOTAL COGS

Simple.

Do not guess your profit. Calculate it.

6.3 WHAT PRODUCTS TO REORDER?

After a few selling rounds (for example, 3 cycles), you will clearly see which products are performing consistently.

You want to identify your top-performing products.

The easiest way:

Seller Central → Reports → Fulfillment → Sales Dashboard

This shows:

- Units sold

- Revenue

- Trends over time

- SKU breakdown

Sort by units sold over a specific time period (30 days, 60 days, etc.) and identify your top performers.

You can also use Business Reports or inventory reports for deeper analysis when you are comfortable.

Bottom line:

- Do not get emotional about products.

- If a product is not performing, discard it.

- Reorder the ones that consistently generate profit within your expected timeframe.

- This model rewards discipline — not attachment.

6.4 OPERATIONAL EXPENSES

You will have monthly operational expenses such as:

- Amazon Professional account ($39.99/month – automatically deducted from your sales)
- Product research tools (Helium 10, Jungle Scout, Keepa, Analyzer Tools, etc.)
- Amazon insurance (mandatory)
- Repricer software
- Accounting software (Xero/QuickBooks, etc.)
- Domain & website hosting
- Virtual office and phone
- Professional email

It may seem like a lot.

Be strict.

Do not purchase tools just because they "make life easier."

Question every dollar.

Keep operational expenses lean.

As a general guideline:

- If you are under $20,000/month revenue → keep expenses under 3%

- If you are between $20,000–$50,000/month → keep under 7%

Discipline in expenses protects your profit.

For detailed operational expense templates, you can find additional training at www.ebusinessmastery.com.

6.5 KNOW YOUR NUMBERS

Yes, you want to know exactly how much profit you are making. We discussed how to calculate that.

But before reinvesting or injecting more money into your business, understand this:

- Do not grow for the sake of growing.

- Once you have completed several rounds, you will start noticing patterns in your ASIN performance.

- This model is designed to be predictable.

For example:

You have 20 replenishable ASINs generating $2,000 gross profit per month.

That means each ASIN averages around $100/month.

Now calculate your "Magic Number."

This is the number you need monthly to maintain your lifestyle (for example, your current job income).

Let's say your magic number is $5,000/month.

Your growth path becomes:

20 ASINs → $2,000/month

50 ASINs → $5,000/month

That means adding 30 similar, validated ASINs.

How did you reach 20 ASINs?

You already know.

Follow the same process.

Growth in this model is not random.

It is strategic.

It is intentional.

It is predictable — if you follow the system correctly.

Do not grow blindly, grow with numbers.

CHAPTER 7

FINAL WORDS

7.1 PAY YOURSELF FIRST

You may have heard this before — and I completely agree with this concept.

That's why I want to emphasize it in this final chapter of my book.

As a business owner, you might think you are the last person who should get paid from your business.

But the truth is, if you pay yourself last, you will always feel stressed, thinking your business is not making enough — even when it actually can afford to pay you.

You reinvest everything.

You increase revenue.

You burn out.

You never feel progress.

Over time, you subconsciously create a negative association with your business.

And what do you think happens long term?

Not good.

The trick is to pay yourself first.

When you do that, you create a positive meaning around your business in your mind. Everything else begins to fall into place.

You might ask:

How much should I pay myself?

It depends. In the early stages, start with 10%–30% of your net profit. Then work your way up to your "magic number" that we discussed earlier.

There is one caveat.

This only works if you are disciplined with your money and cash flow.

You must know your numbers.

You must be organized.

You must be intentional on payday — for yourself and for your business.

This forces financial discipline.

If you are not paying yourself at all, then what is the point of building a business?

Remember what I said in the beginning.

We do not want to grind all day inside our businesses.

The business must work for us — not the other way around.

7.2 BUILD YOUR TEAM

If you are just starting out, it may feel early to think about building a team.

But if you never think about it, it will never happen.

So think about it now — even if you are not ready yet.

Have you ever wondered how large businesses employ thousands of people?

You might think they have millions of dollars and you do not.

Wrong.

They built their teams strategically over time by allocating a percentage of their revenue toward team building.

If you put aside just 3% of your revenue (for example, $30,000/month), that would be $900/month for your team — and it is tax deductible.

You can hire one or two full-time VAs to handle repetitive tasks such as:

- Analyzing supplier spreadsheets

- Formatting Excel files

- Admin work

- Routine operational tasks

As I said earlier, paying yourself first and then building your team gives you leverage.

Slowly, you begin to enjoy being a true business owner.

7.3 YOU CAN CHANGE YOUR LIFE ONLY IF...

If you have read this book up to this point, I sincerely thank you.

I believe you now have new ideas, inspiration, and a clearer picture of how to build, run, and grow an Amazon business from anywhere in the world.

But here is the honest truth:

Ideas do not change your life.

Theories do not change your life.

Your consistent, directed actions do.

I believe you are one of the few people who will take action — and over time build a business you are proud to own.

7.4 REMEMBER YOUR WHY

At the end of the day, nothing matters if the business you are building is not serving you.

Ask yourself:

- Can it give you freedom to work from anywhere?

- Can you work with people you like?

- Can you work on your own schedule?

- Can you scale it to any level?

- Can it support you financially without you being present all the time?

- Do you work 20% while your systems and team handle 80%?

These are my WHYs.

For me, the answer must be yes to all of them.

I hope you remember your own WHY every day during this journey — and build a solid, long-term business that serves you and your loved ones.

7.5 NEXT STEPS

I enjoy writing and speaking about systems like Amazon FBA that help entrepreneurs build businesses that free them from jobs they do not enjoy or operator roles they cannot escape.

If you found value in this book, please consider leaving a review on Amazon or wherever you purchased it.

Your review helps me continue this mission — to write more and help more people.

If you would like to learn more about Amazon FBA systems and take this further, visit:

www.ebusinessmastery.com

Sincerely,

Mahin

WANT MORE TIPS AND GUIDANCE ON HOW TO MAKE YOUR AMAZON STOREFRONT SUCCESSFUL?

SIGN UP FOR MY IN-DEPTH ONLINE COURSE AT EBUSINESSMASTERY.COM/BOOK OR SCAN THE QR CODE TO LEARN MORE.

NOTES

1. 81.9% Small businesses have no employees.SBA, Small Business Administration USA, FAQ, 19 Feb, 2026.
   https://advocacy.sba.gov/wp-content/uploads/2024/12/Frequently-Asked-Questions-About-Small-Business_2024-508.pdf

2. Scale Suite, "Australian Business Statistics 2026: SME Revenue, Growth & Industry Data" www.scalesuite.com.au, Dec 2025 https://www.scalesuite.com.au/resources/australian-business-statistics

3. FSB, "Business Population Estimates for the UK and Regions in 2025, " www.fsb.org.uk, 19th Feb, 2026, https://www.fsb.org.uk/media-centre/uk-small-business-statistics#:~:text=Composition%20of%20the%20business%20population,of%20the%20estimated%20total%20population.

4. 9-figure Amazon sellers Marketplace Pulse,
    "100,000 Million-Dollar Amazon Sellers"
    www.marketplacepulse.com, 24 Jul, 2025
    https://www.marketplacepulse.com/articles/100000-
    million-dollar-amazon-sellers?

5. Marketplace selling partner contribution to
    Amazon's revenue Marketplace Pulse, "Amazon
    GMV Surpassed $800 Billion in 2025"
    www.marketplacepulse.com, 06 Feb, 2026
    https://www.marketplacepulse.com/articles/amazon
    -gmv-surpassed-800-billion-in-2025

6. Amazon active customers Capital One, "Amazon
    Statistics," capitaloneshopping.com, 28 Jan, 2026
    https://capitaloneshopping.com/research/amazon-
    statistics/